Wash Day

by
Sydnie Meltzer
Kleinhenz

illustrated by
Michael
Chesworth

Scott Foresman

Editorial Offices: Glenview, Illinois • New York, New York
Sales Offices: Reading, Massachusetts • Duluth, Georgia
Glenview, Illinois • Carrollton, Texas • Menlo Park, California

I got the soap.

I got the tub.

I got my bike.

Rub, rub, rub.
Looking good!
Looking so good!

5

Pam came out.

She saw the tub.

Pam went in.

She got her bike.

Rub, rub, rub.

Looking good!

Looking so good!

Mama came out.

She saw the tub.

Mama went in.

She got the chairs.

Rub, rub, rub.
Looking good!
Looking so good!

Papa came out.

He saw the tub.

He got the car.

Rub, rub, rub.
Looking good!
Looking so good!
Look at us!

What a mess!

Now we have to wash.

Looking good!